**HAL LEONARD
STUDENT
PIANO
LIBRARY**

Classical Th[...]

Favorite orchestral works arranged for piano solo
by Fred Kern, Phillip Keveren, and Mona Rejino

Text Author
Barbara Kreader

Editor
Margaret Otwell

Classical Themes Level 3 is designed for use with the third book of any piano method.

Concepts in *Classical Themes Level 3*:

Range

Symbols

pp, p, mp, mf, f, ff, ♯, ♭, ♮, *ritard, a tempo,*
D.S. al Fine, To Coda ⊕, *8va, loco,*

simple pedaling

Rhythm

time signatures: 2/4, 4/4, 3/4

Intervals

2nd, 3rd, 4th, 5th, 6th
melodic and harmonic

To access audio visit:
www.halleonard.com/mylibrary

3843-0114-8766-1856

ISBN 978-1-4950-4760-2

**HAL•LEONARD®
CORPORATION**

7777 W. BLUEMOUND RD. P.O. BOX 13819 MILWAUKEE, WI 53213

In Australia Contact:
Hal Leonard Australia Pty. Ltd.
4 Lentara Court
Cheltenham, Victoria, 3192 Australia
Email: ausadmin@halleonard.com.au

Visit Hal Leonard Online at
www.halleonard.com

Table of Contents

About the Compositions

Waltz from the operetta THE MERRY WIDOW
Franz Lehár (1870-1948)

The Austro-Hungarian composer Franz Lehár earned the honor of being the leading operetta (small-scale opera) composer of the early 20th century. The easy flow of his melodies, with their unexpected turns and fluid phrasing, gave his operetta music a substance not found in that of other composers in this genre. His 1905 operetta, *The Merry Widow*, is an engaging story full of romance and wit, reality and fantasy. Lehár's music is generally more serious than the music of other operettas. Nonetheless, he used elements from the blues and characteristics of the foxtrot, tango, and skinny – popular new dances of his time – in his music. His waltzes, such as this one, were an important part of the story's action rather than mere interludes. *The Merry Widow* filled Viennese opera houses and became the greatest success in operetta history.

Trumpet Tune
Henry Purcell (c.1659-1695)

The English composer Henry Purcell started his musical career as a chorister in the Chapel Royal. In 1682, Purcell was appointed church organist at Chapel Royal. Though only 23 years old, he was already a popular author of fantasias, anthems, and theater songs. Considered a genius in his day, his operas, such as *Dido and Aeneas* (1688) and *The Fairy Queen* (1692) were popular hits. He wrote anthems for the coronation of James II in 1685, and for Queen Mary's funeral in 1694. He was routinely asked to compose odes – songs of welcome that marked important events – such as St. Cecilia's Day, or the return of the king to London. Yet Purcell's music fell into neglect and was not revived until the end of the 19th century. This *Trumpet Tune* has survived as an enduring favorite.

Lullaby Opus 49, No. 4 "Wiegenlied"
Johannes Brahms (1833-1897)

According to legend, the German composer Johannes Brahms slept like a baby, but snored so loudly that no one could sleep in the same room with him! Yet mothers have hummed his *Lullaby* to babies for nearly two centuries. Often, it is the first classical music children hear. Brahms, who thought folk songs were an ideal musical form, arranged many German folk songs, including a set of fourteen dedicated to the children of Robert and Clara Schumann. He wrote this charming *Lullaby* in a folk-song style.

Turkish March from THE RUINS OF ATHENS
Ludwig van Beethoven (1770-1827)

The German composer Ludwig van Beethoven composed dramatic, powerful music that matched his personality. His compositions sound more roughhewn and less melodic than those of Haydn and Mozart. During the 18th century, the exotic, jingling, percussive sound of Turkish music enjoyed great popularity. Mozart and Haydn were also influenced by the bands of Turkish musicians who roamed the streets of Vienna playing their cymbals, bass drum and triangle. Beethoven even added Turkish percussion to his famous *Ninth Symphony!*

Entr'acte from ROSAMUNDE
Franz Schubert (1797-1828)

Rosamunde, Princess of Cyprus, a Romance by the now-forgotten Austrian playwright Helmine von Chezy, lasted only two performances. Yet the Viennese composer Franz Schubert's glorious incidental music for the play's far-fetched plot lives on. Incidental music, much like today's movie music, prepares and ends scenes in a play, creating mood and atmosphere, linking acts, and providing cover for scene changes. Instead of the recorded soundtrack we hear in movies, orchestras in Schubert's time sat in a "pit" in front of and below the stage and played the music live.

La donna è mobile from the opera RIGOLETTO
Giuseppe Verdi (1813-1901)

The Italian composer Giuseppi Verdi wrote supercharged operas for most of his very long life. His operas unfold the human drama of their characters in melodramatic, nearly unbelievable plots, which are often full of political intrigue. *Rigoletto* tells the story of the Duke of Mantua, who, disguised as a student, romances Gilda, daughter of the court jester, Rigoletto. The Duke is not an especially honorable man, and he sings *La donna è mobile (Woman Is Fickle, Changeable Like A Feather In The Wind)* several times throughout the opera. At first it sounds like a carefree comment on the difficulties of loving a woman. But in the final act, as Gilda sacrifices her life to spare the life of the Duke, the music takes on a much darker meaning.

Theme from SCHEHERAZADE
Nicolai Rimsky-Korsakov (1844-1908)

The Russian composer Rimsky-Korsakov wrote the music for the symphonic suite, *Scheherazade*. Based on *The Tales of One Thousand and One Nights*, *Scheherazade* tells the story of a young woman married to a bad-tempered Sultan, who cheats her own death by telling the Sultan stories each night. They intrigue him so much that he spares her life to hear just one more tale. Rimsky-Korsakov's music, with its vivid orchestral colors, matches the exotic nature of the stories, each one more fantastic than the last.

Theme from SYMPHONY NO. 1
Johannes Brahms (1833-1897)

The world expected a symphony from the young German composer Johannes Brahms, so he felt obligated to write one. In 1870 he wrote: *"I shall never write a symphony. You don't know what it means to be dogged by that giant (Beethoven)."* Because Brahms feared he would fail to match the standards Beethoven set, it took him longer to compose his first symphony than to write any other work. His dear friend Clara Schumann continually encouraged him through the long process. In one of her many letters to Brahms, she wrote: *"Men like you lie in wait for the charms of Nature and so derive nourishment from the soul... such a sky of storm may lead to a symphony."*

Polovetsian Dance from the opera PRINCE IGOR
Alexander Borodin (1833-1887)

The Russian composer Alexander Borodin combined the careers of composer and physician. He founded a School of Medicine for Women and still found time to begin an opera, *Prince Igor*. The Russian composers Rimsky-Korsakov and Glazunov completed it for him after he died. The opera tells the tale of Prince Igor and the Russian army, who are fighting the Polovetsi. During Act III, the Polovetsi are winning, and they celebrate their victory by drinking and dancing *(Polovetsian Dances)* themselves into a stupor. Prince Igor and his army use this unguarded opportunity to steal away from the battlefront and return home.

The Elephant from CARNIVAL OF THE ANIMALS
Camille Saint-Saëns (1835-1921)

The French composer Camille Saint-Saëns' suite, *Carnival of the Animals* (1886) mimics the sounds and movements of several animals: swans, elephants, lions, and even pianists! Saint-Saëns originally wrote this suite for a small chamber ensemble that included two pianos, and later arranged it for a large-scale orchestra. He publicly disavowed its enormous popularity, claiming he'd only written the work as a moment's diversion. The poet Ogden Nash later wrote humorous poetry for each piece. Today, performances of *Carnival of the Animals* often include a narrator, who reads Nash's witty, poetic animal characterizations before the musical entrance of each animal.

The Merry Widow Waltz

from the operetta THE MERRY WIDOW

Franz Lehár (1870 - 1948)
Austria
Originally for orchestra
Arranged by Mona Rejino

Accompaniment (Student plays one octave higher than written.)

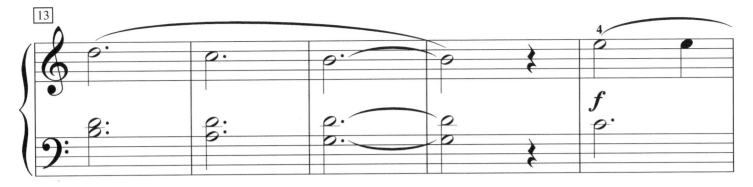

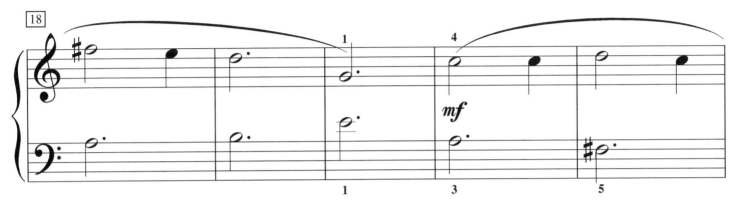

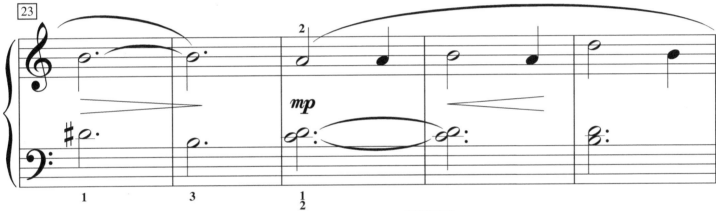

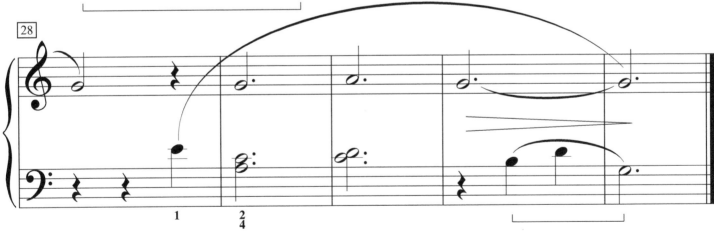

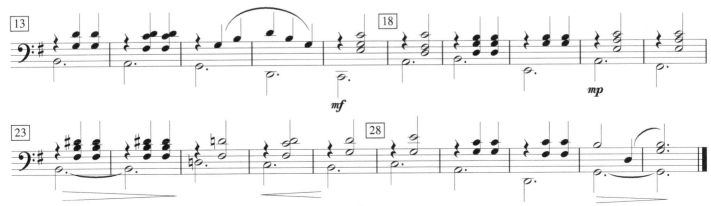

Trumpet Tune

Henry Purcell (1659 - 1695)
England
Originally for organ
Arranged by Mona Rejino

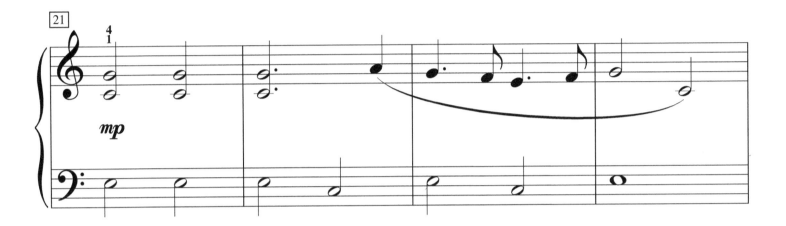

Lullaby

Opus 49, No. 4
"Wiegenlied"

Johannes Brahms (1833 - 1897)
Germany
Originally for voice and piano
Arranged by Phillip Keveren

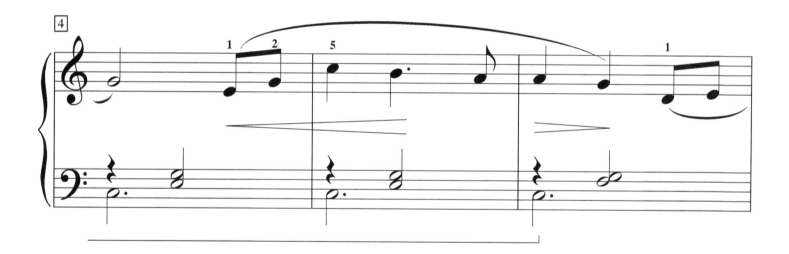

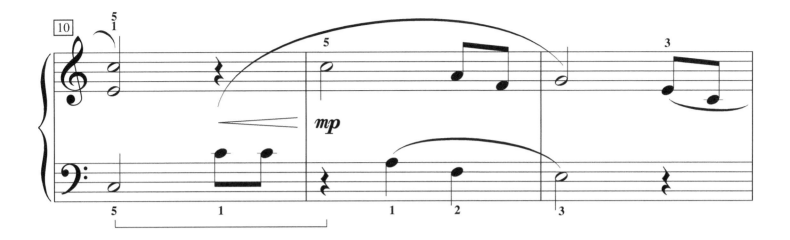

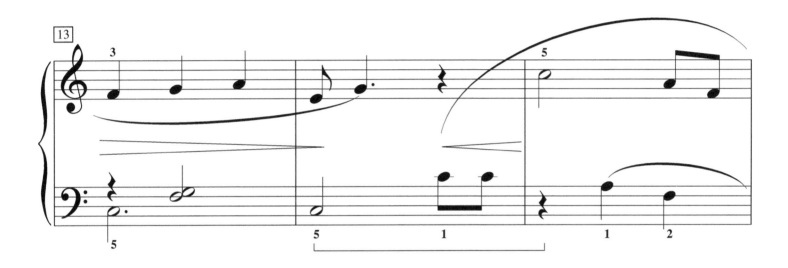

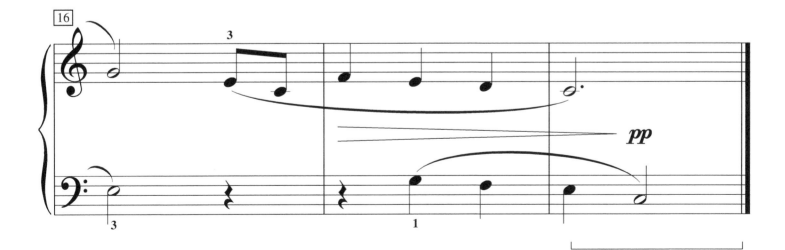

Turkish March
from THE RUINS OF ATHENS

Ludwig van Beethoven (1770 - 1827)
Germany/Austria
Originally for orchestra
Arranged by Fred Kern

Lively (♩ = 138)

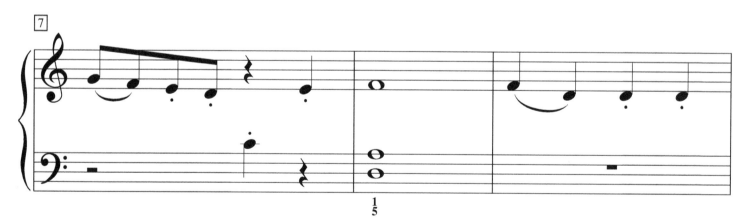

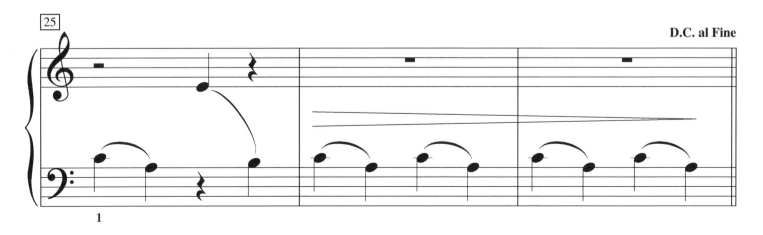

13

Entr'acte
from ROSAMUNDE

Franz Schubert (1797 - 1828)
Austria
Originally for orchestra
Arranged by Phillip Keveren

Andantino (♩ = 84)

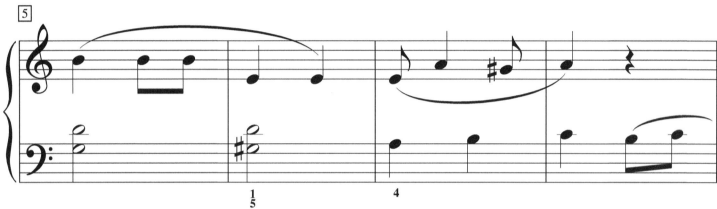

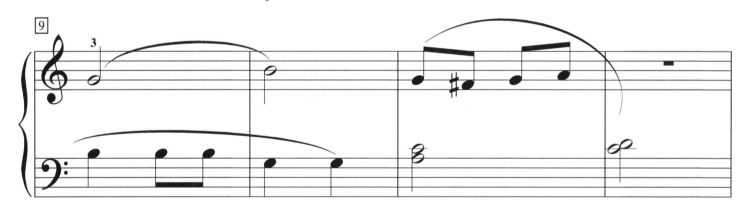

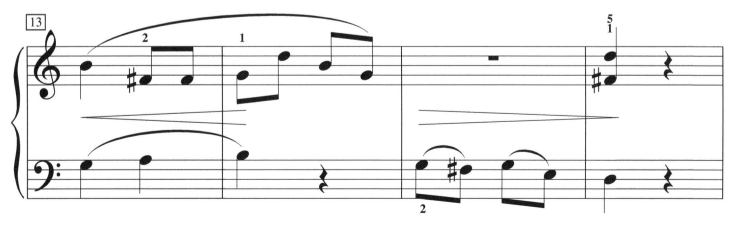

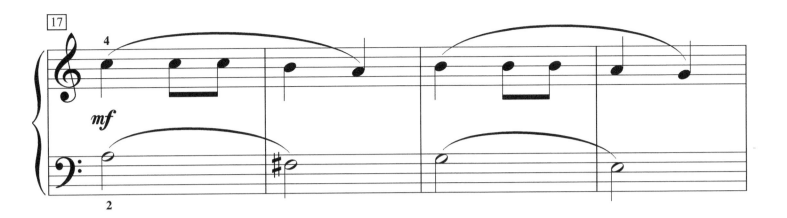

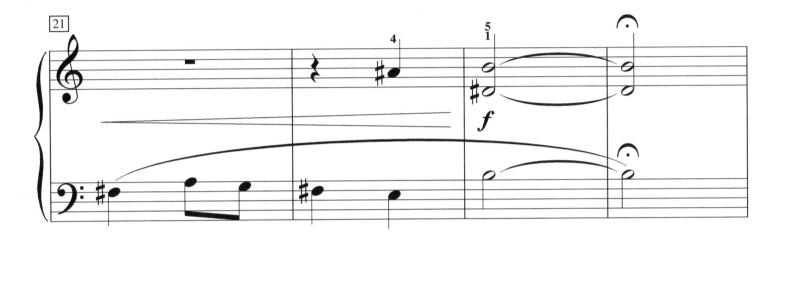

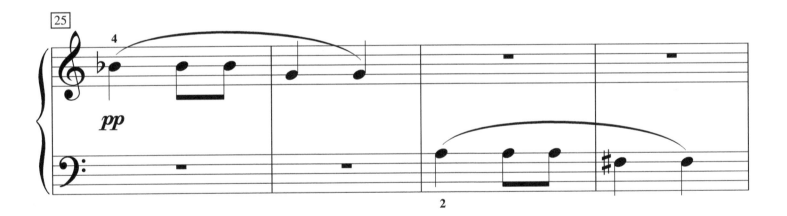

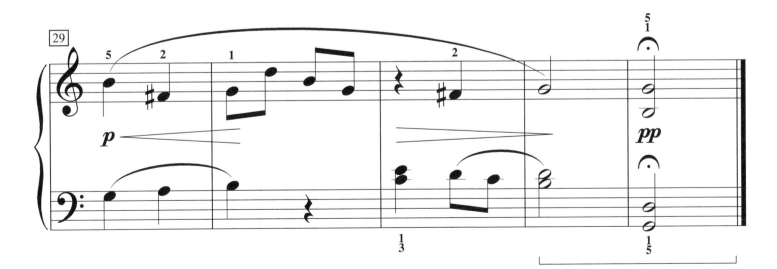

La donna è mobile

from the opera RIGOLETTO

Giuseppe Verdi (1813 - 1901)
Italy
Originally for voice and orchestra
Arranged by Mona Rejino

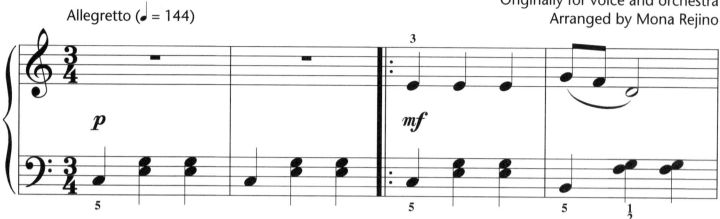

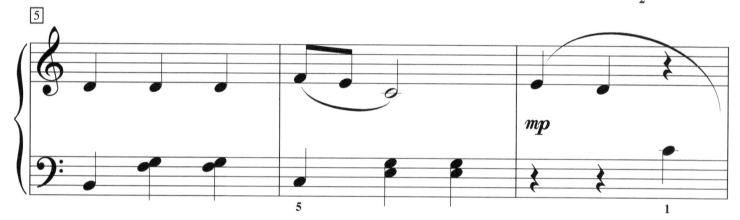

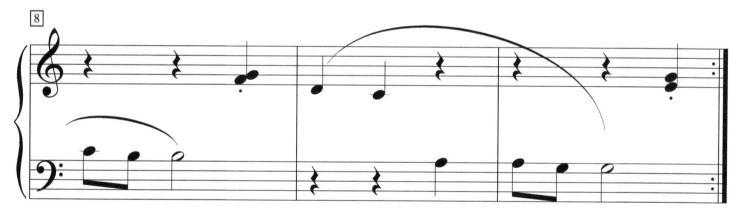

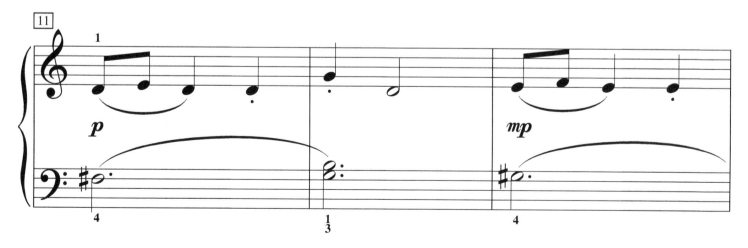

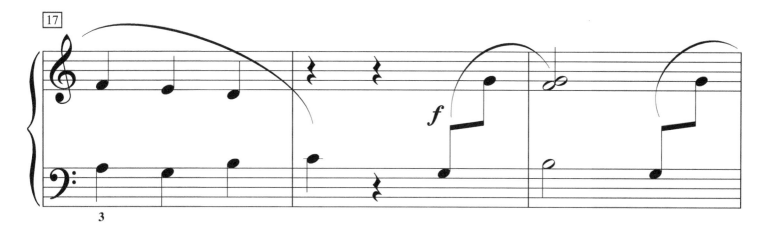

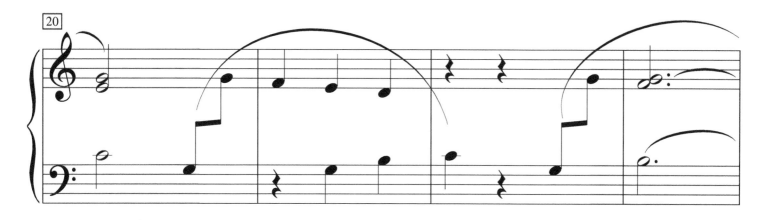

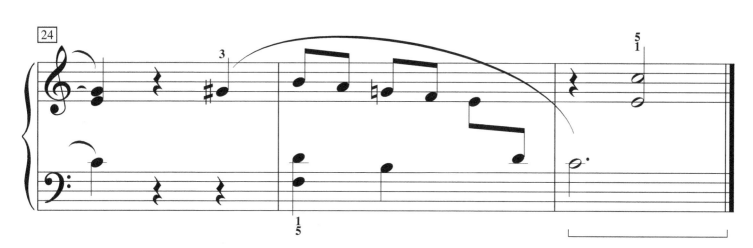

Scheherazade
Theme from Part Three

Nicolai Rimsky-Korsakov (1844 - 1908)
Russia
Originally for orchestra
Arranged by Mona Rejino

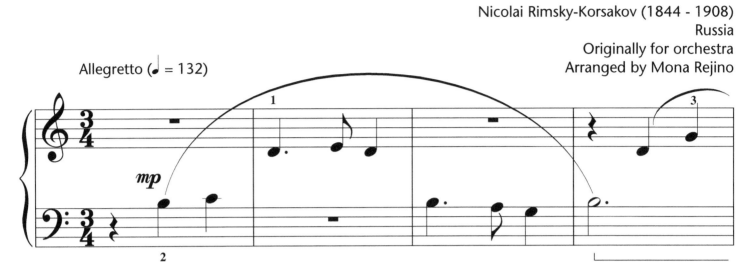

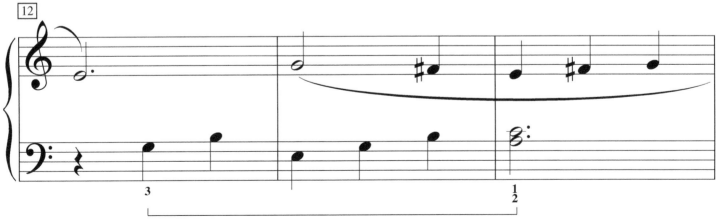

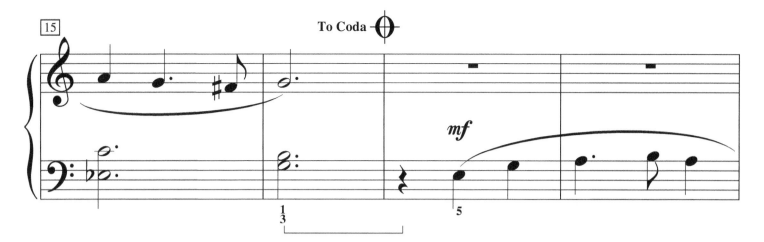

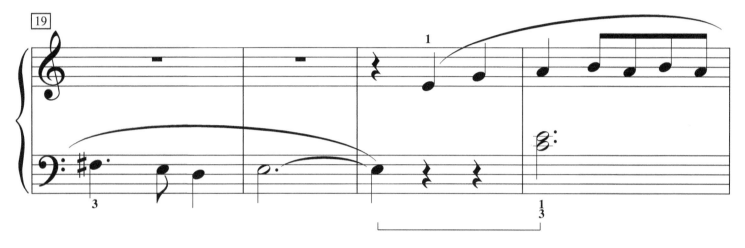

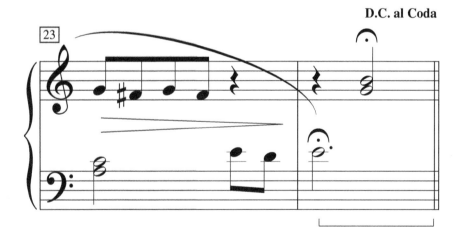

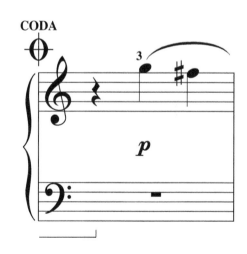

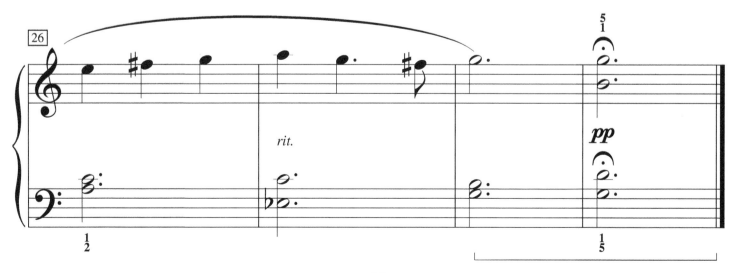

Symphony No. 1
Fourth Movement Theme

Johannes Brahms (1833 - 1897)
Germany
Originally for orchestra
Arranged by Fred Kern

Allegro (♩ = 112)

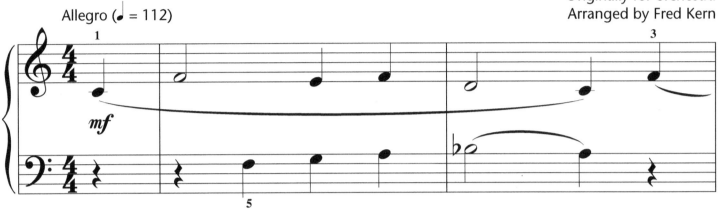

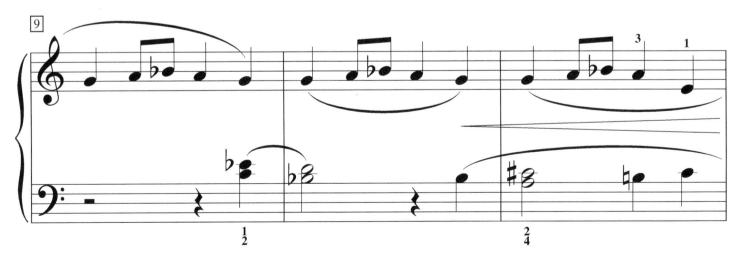

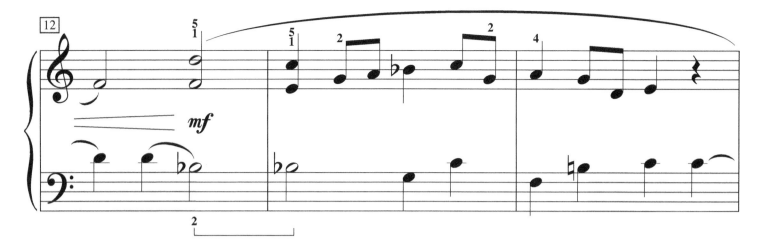

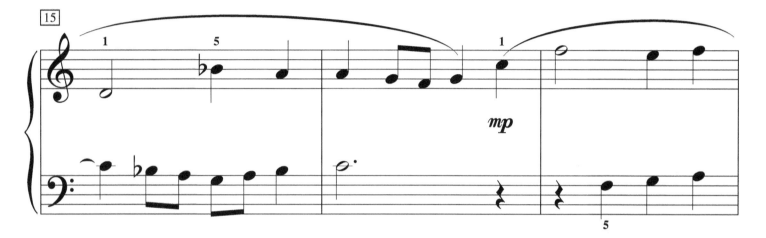

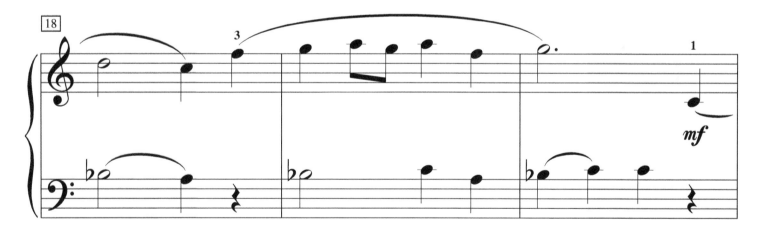

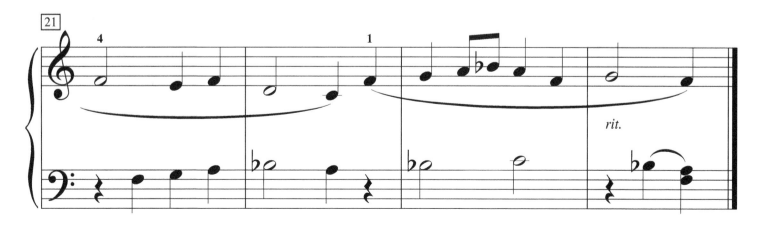

Polovetsian Dance

from the opera PRINCE IGOR

First Theme

Alexander Borodin (1833 - 1887)
Russia
Originally for orchestra
Arranged by Phillip Keveren

Andantino (♩ = 116)

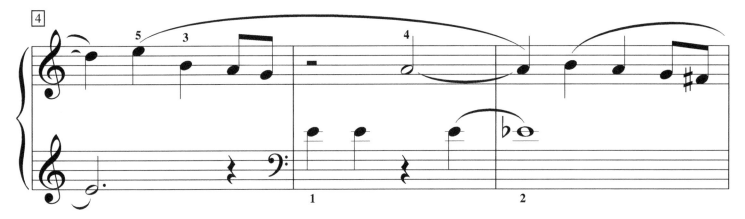

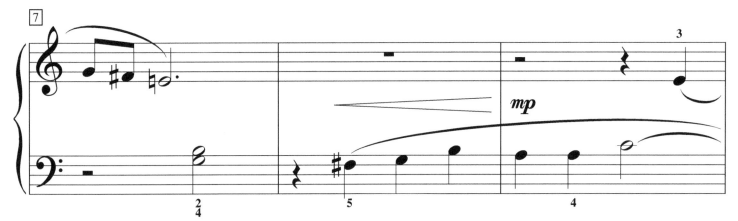

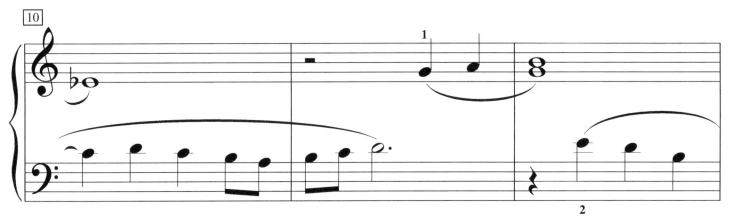

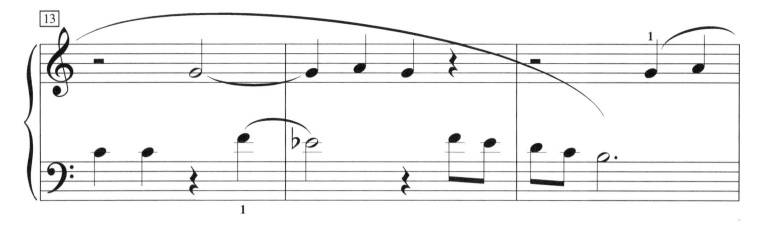

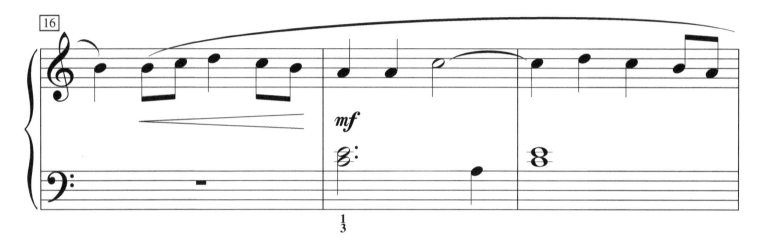

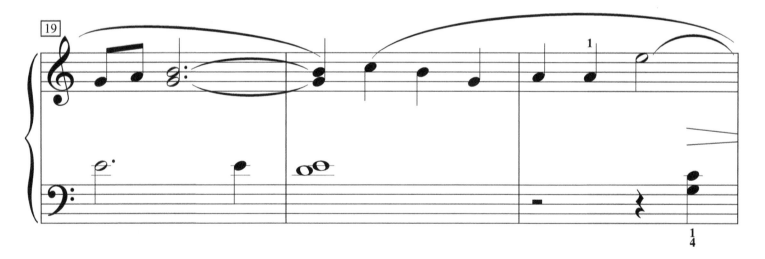

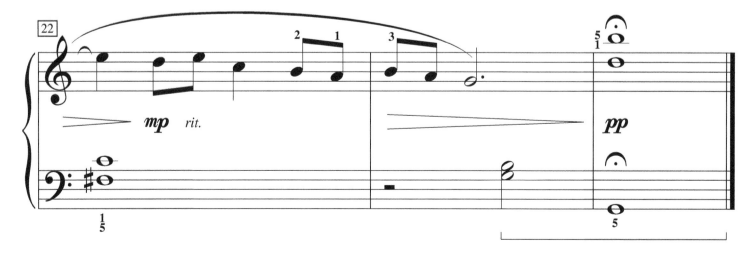

The Elephant

"L'eléphant"
from CARNIVAL OF THE ANIMALS

Camille Saint-Saëns (1835 - 1921)
France
Originally for chamber ensemble
Arranged by Fred Kern

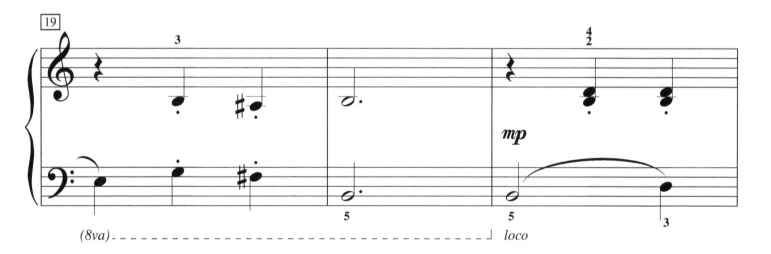

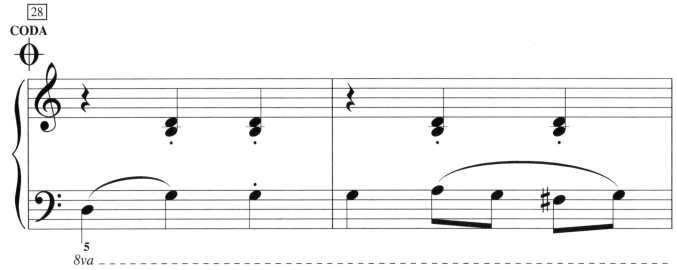

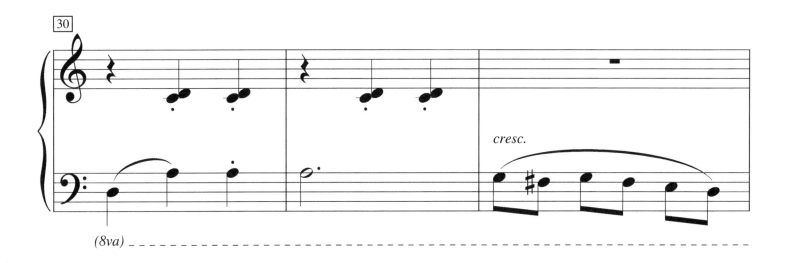

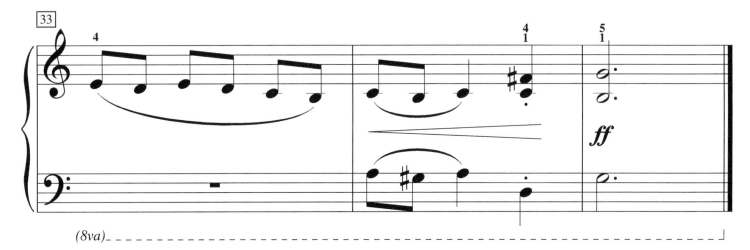

THE MIDDLE AGES

400 AD	600	800	1000	1200	1400

MUSIC

During the Middle Ages (also called the *Medieval Period*), the Roman Catholic church was the most powerful influence in European life. The church's music was a collection of ancient melodies called *plainsong* or *chant*, sung in unison (single line) with Latin words. The chants were organized in about 600 AD by Pope Gregory, and these official versions are known as *Gregorian chant*. Later, simple harmonies were added, and eventually the harmony parts became independent melodies sung with the main tune. This is called *polyphony*. Church music was written down using *neumes*, or square notes.

Outside the churches, traveling entertainers called *troubadours* or *minstrels* would sing songs about life and love in the language of the scommon people. This music was more lively and would often be accompanied by a drum, a wooden flute or an early form of the guitar called a *lute*.

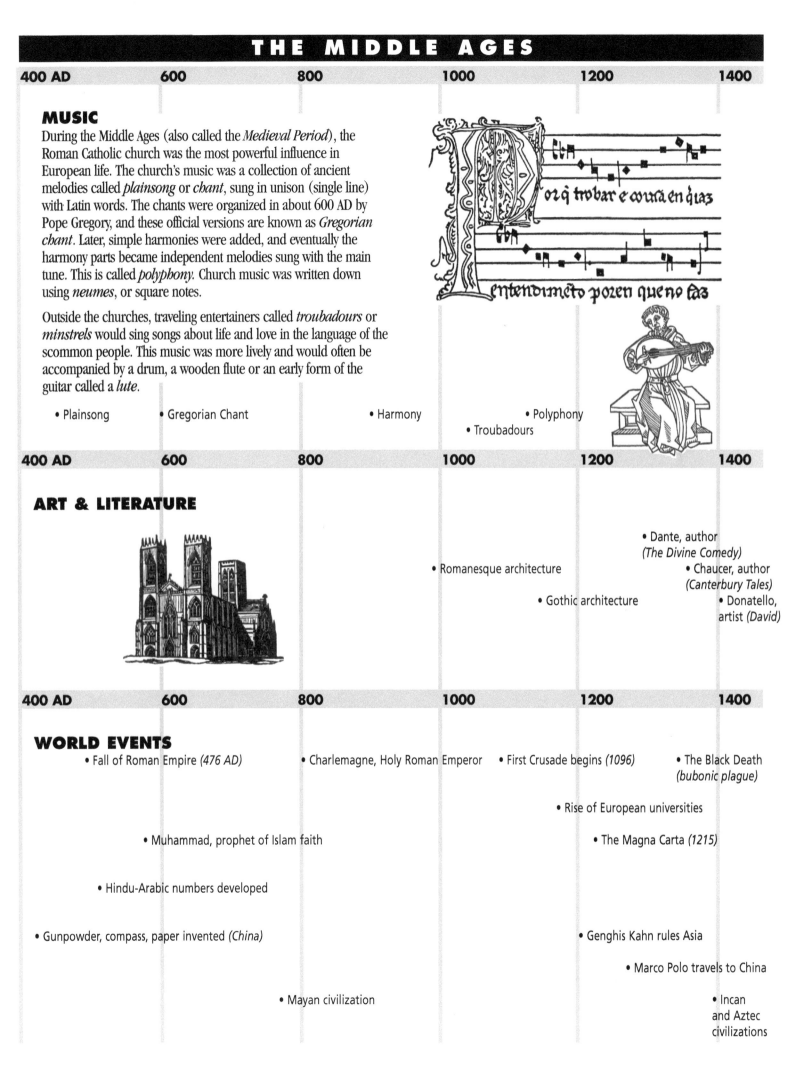

- Plainsong
- Gregorian Chant
- Harmony
- Polyphony
- Troubadours

400 AD	600	800	1000	1200	1400

ART & LITERATURE

- Romanesque architecture
- Gothic architecture
- Dante, author *(The Divine Comedy)*
- Chaucer, author *(Canterbury Tales)*
- Donatello, artist *(David)*

400 AD	600	800	1000	1200	1400

WORLD EVENTS

- Fall of Roman Empire *(476 AD)*
- Charlemagne, Holy Roman Emperor
- First Crusade begins *(1096)*
- The Black Death *(bubonic plague)*
- Rise of European universities
- Muhammad, prophet of Islam faith
- The Magna Carta *(1215)*
- Hindu-Arabic numbers developed
- Gunpowder, compass, paper invented *(China)*
- Genghis Kahn rules Asia
- Marco Polo travels to China
- Mayan civilization
- Incan and Aztec civilizations

1450	1500	1550	1600

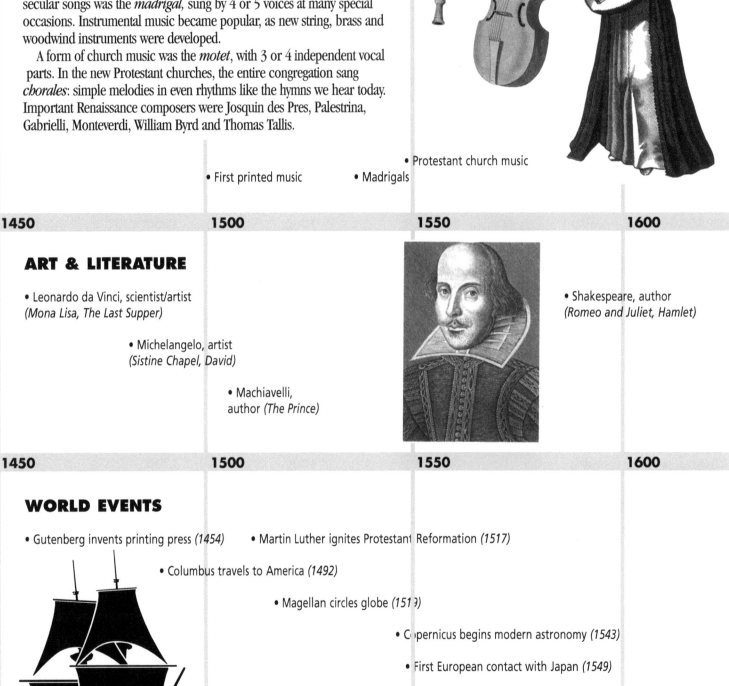

MUSIC

The era from about 1450–1600 was called the *Renaissance* ("rebirth") because people wanted to recreate the artistic and scientific glories of ancient Greece and Rome. It was also a time of discovery. The new printing press brought music to the homes of the growing middle class. European society became more *secular*, or non-religious, and concerts were featured in the halls of the nobility. An entertaining form of secular songs was the *madrigal*, sung by 4 or 5 voices at many special occasions. Instrumental music became popular, as new string, brass and woodwind instruments were developed.

A form of church music was the *motet*, with 3 or 4 independent vocal parts. In the new Protestant churches, the entire congregation sang *chorales*: simple melodies in even rhythms like the hymns we hear today. Important Renaissance composers were Josquin des Pres, Palestrina, Gabrielli, Monteverdi, William Byrd and Thomas Tallis.

• Protestant church music

• First printed music   • Madrigals

1450	1500	1550	1600

ART & LITERATURE

• Leonardo da Vinci, scientist/artist
(*Mona Lisa, The Last Supper*)

• Michelangelo, artist
(*Sistine Chapel, David*)

• Machiavelli,
author (*The Prince*)

• Shakespeare, author
(*Romeo and Juliet, Hamlet*)

1450	1500	1550	1600

WORLD EVENTS

• Gutenberg invents printing press (*1454*)   • Martin Luther ignites Protestant Reformation (*1517*)

• Columbus travels to America (*1492*)

• Magellan circles globe (*1519*)

• Copernicus begins modern astronomy (*1543*)

• First European contact with Japan (*1549*)

| 1600 | 1650 | 1700 | 1750 |

MUSIC

Music and the arts (and even clothing) became fancier and more dramatic in the *Baroque* era (about 1600-1750). Like the fancy decorations of Baroque church architecture, melodies were often played with *grace notes*, or quick nearby tones added to decorate them. Rhythms became more complex with time signatures, bar lines and faster-moving melodic lines. Our now familiar major and minor scales formed the basis for harmony, and chords were standardized to what we often hear today.

The harpsichord became the most popular keyboard instrument, with players often *improvising* (making up) their parts using the composer's chords and bass line. Violin making reached new heights in Italy. Operas, ballets and small orchestras were beginning to take shape, as composers specified the exact instruments, tempos and dynamics to be performed.

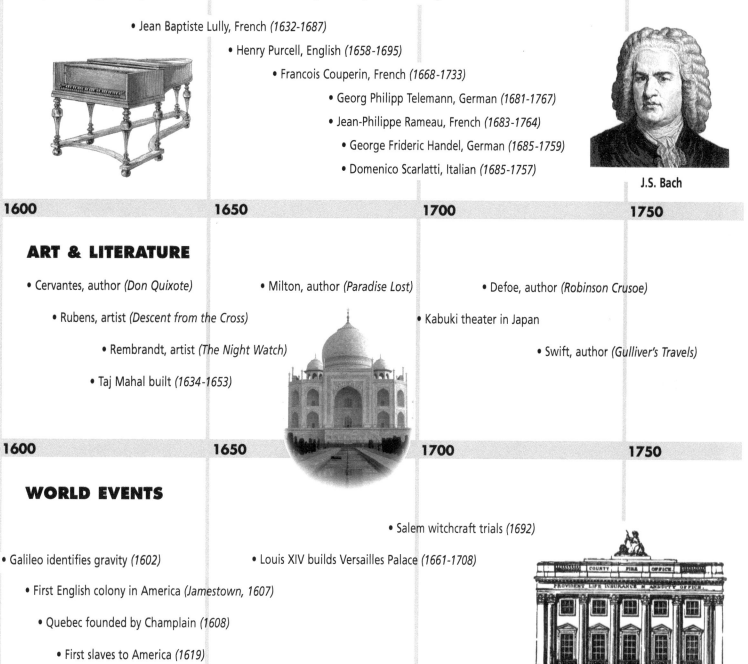

- Jean Baptiste Lully, French *(1632-1687)*
- Henry Purcell, English *(1658-1695)*
- Francois Couperin, French *(1668-1733)*
- Georg Philipp Telemann, German *(1681-1767)*
- Jean-Philippe Rameau, French *(1683-1764)*
- George Frideric Handel, German *(1685-1759)*
- Domenico Scarlatti, Italian *(1685-1757)*

J.S. Bach

| 1600 | 1650 | 1700 | 1750 |

ART & LITERATURE

- Cervantes, author *(Don Quixote)*
- Rubens, artist *(Descent from the Cross)*
- Rembrandt, artist *(The Night Watch)*
- Taj Mahal built *(1634-1653)*

- Milton, author *(Paradise Lost)*

- Defoe, author *(Robinson Crusoe)*
- Kabuki theater in Japan
- Swift, author *(Gulliver's Travels)*

| 1600 | 1650 | 1700 | 1750 |

WORLD EVENTS

- Salem witchcraft trials *(1692)*
- Galileo identifies gravity *(1602)*
- Louis XIV builds Versailles Palace *(1661-1708)*
- First English colony in America *(Jamestown, 1607)*
- Quebec founded by Champlain *(1608)*
- First slaves to America *(1619)*

- Isaac Newton *(1642-1727)* formulates principals of physics and math

1750 | **1775** | **1800** | **1820**

MUSIC

The *Classical* era, from about 1750 to the early 1800's, was a time of great contrasts. While patriots fought for the rights of the common people in the American and French revolutions, composers were employed to entertain wealthy nobles and aristocrats. Music became simpler and more elegant, with melodies often flowing over accompaniment patterns in regular 4-bar phrases. Like the architecture of ancient *Classical* Greece, music was fit together in "building blocks" by balancing one phrase against another, or one entire section against another.

The piano replaced the harpsichord and became the most popular instrument for the *concerto* (solo) with orchestra accompaniment. The string quartet became the favorite form of *chamber* (small group) music, and orchestra concerts featured *symphonies* (longer compositions with 4 contrasting parts or *movements*). Toward the end of this era, Beethoven's changing musical style led the way toward the more emotional and personal expression of Romantic music.

Haydn

Beethoven

Mozart

- Franz Haydn, Austrian (German) *(1732-1809)*
- Johann Christian Bach, German *(1735-1782)*
- Muzio Clementi, Italian *(1752-1832)*
- Wolfgang Amadeus Mozart, German *(1756-1791)*

- Ludwig van Beethoven, German *(1770-1827)*
- Antonio Diabelli, Italian *(1781-1858)*
- Friedrich Kuhlau, German *(1786-1832)*

1750 | **1775** | **1800** | **1820**

ART & LITERATURE

- Samuel Johnson, author *(Dictionary)*

- Voltaire, author *(Candide)*

- Gainsborough, artist *(The Blue Boy)*

- *Encyclopedia Britannica*, first edition

- Wm. Wordsworth, author *(Lyrical Ballads)*

- Goethe, author *(Faust)*

- Goya, artist *(Witch's Sabbath)*

- Jane Austen, author *(Pride and Prejudice)*

1750 | **1775** | **1800** | **1820**

WORLD EVENTS

- Ben Franklin discovers electricity *(1751)*

- American Revolution *(1775-1783)*

- French Revolution *(1789-1794)*

- Napoleon crowned Emperor of France *(1804)*

- Lewis and Clark explore northwest *(1804)*

- Metronome invented *(1815)*

- First steamship crosses Atlantic *(1819)*

THE ROMANTIC ERA

| 1820 | 1840 | 1860 | 1880 | 1900 |

MUSIC

The last compositions of Beethoven were among the first of the new *Romantic* era, lasting from the early 1800's to about 1900. No longer employed by churches or nobles, composers became free from Classical restraints and expressed their personal emotions through their music. Instead of simple titles like *Concerto* or *Symphony*, they would often add descriptive titles like *Witches' Dance* or *To The New World*. Orchestras became larger, including nearly all the standard instruments we now use. Composers began to write much more difficult and complex music, featuring more "colorful" instrument combinations and harmonies.

Nationalism was an important trend in this era. Composers used folk music and folk legends (especially in Russia, eastern Europe and Scandinavia) to identify their music with their native lands. Today's concert audiences still generally prefer the drama of Romantic music to any other kind.

Schumann

Brahms

- Franz Schubert, German *(1797-1828)*
- Felix Mendelssohn, German *(1809-1847)*
- Friedrich Burgmuller, German *(1806-1874)*
- Frederic Francois Chopin, Polish *(1810-1849)*
- Robert Schumann, German *(1810-1856)*
- Franz Liszt, Hungarian *(1811-1886)*
- Stephen Heller, German *(1813-1888)*
- Fritz Spindler, German *(1817-1905)*

- Cornelius Gurlitt, German *(1820-1901)*
- Cesar Auguste Franck, French *(1822-1890)*
- Johannes Brahms, German *(1833-1897)*
- Camille Saint-Saens, French *(1835-1921)*
- Modest Mussorgsky, Russian *(1839-1881)*
- Peter Ilyich Tchaikovsky, Russian *(1840-1893)*
- Edvard Grieg, Norwegian *(1844-1908)*

| 1820 | 1840 | 1860 | 1880 | 1900 |

ART & LITERATURE

- Vincent van Gogh, artist *(The Sunflowers)*

- Charles Dickens, author *(The Pickwick Papers, David Copperfield)*

- Lewis Carroll, author *(Alice In Wonderland)*

- Rudyard Kipling, author *(Jungle Book)*

- Pierre Renoir, artist *(Luncheon of the Boating Party)*

- Louisa May Alcott, author *(Little Women)*

- Harriet Beecher Stowe, author *(Uncle Tom's Cabin)*

- Jules Verne, author *(20,000 Leagues Under The Sea)*
- Claude Monet, artist *(Gare Saint-Lazare)*

- Mark Twain, author *(Tom Sawyer, Huckleberry Finn)*

| 1820 | 1840 | 1860 | 1880 | 1900 |

WORLD EVENTS

- First railroad *(1830)*

- American Civil War *(1861-1865)*

- Samuel Morse invents telegraph *(1837)*

- First photography *(1838)*

- Alexander Graham Bell invents telephone *(1876)*

- Edison invents phonograph, practical light bulb, movie projector *(1877-1888)*

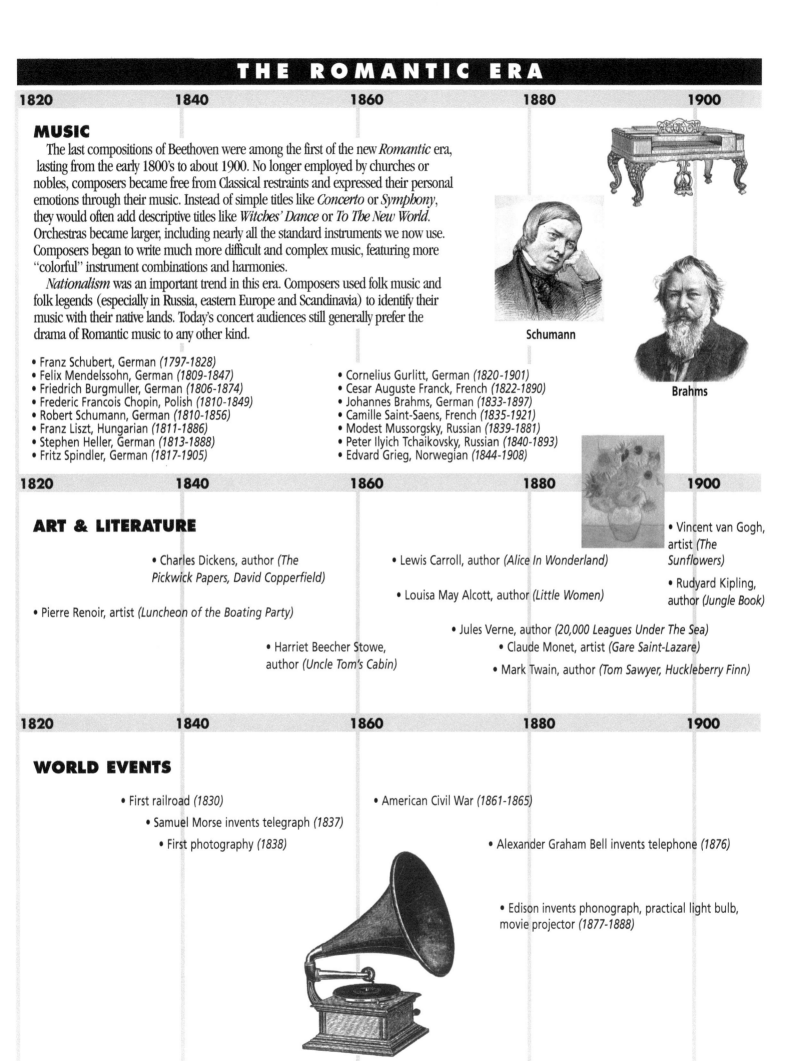

31

| 1900 | 1925 | 1950 | 1975 | 2000 |

- Edward MacDowell, American *(1861-1908)*
- Claude Debussy, French *(1862-1918)*
- Alexander Scriabin, Russian *(1872-1915)*
- Sergei Rachmaninoff, Russian *(1873-1943)*
- Arnold Schoenberg, German *(1874-1950)*
- Maurice Ravel, French *(1875-1937)*
- Bela Bartok, Hungarian *(1881-1945)*
- Heitor Villa-Lobos, Brazilian *(1881-1959)*
- Igor Stravinsky, Russian *(1882-1971)*
- Sergei Prokofieff, Russian *(1891-1952)*
- Paul Hindemith, German *(1895-1963)*
- George Gershwin, American *(1898-1937)*
- Aaron Copland, American *(1900-1990)*
- Aram Khachaturian, Russian *(1903-1978)*
- Dmitri Kabalevsky, Russian *(1904-1986)*
- Dmitri Shostakovich, Russian *(1906-1975)*
- Samuel Barber, American *(1910-1981)*
- Norman Dello Joio, American *(1913-   )*
- Vincent Persichetti, American *(1915-1987)*
- Philip Glass, American *(1937-   )*

MUSIC

The *20th century* was a diverse era of new ideas that "broke the rules" of traditional music. Styles of music moved in many different directions.

Impressionist composers Debussy and Ravel wrote music that seems more vague and blurred than the Romantics. New slightly-dissonant chords were used, and like Impressionist paintings, much of their music describes an impression of nature.

Composer Arnold Schoenberg devised a way to throw away all the old ideas of harmony by creating *12-tone* music. All 12 tones of the chromatic scale were used equally, with no single pitch forming a "key center."

Some of the music of Stravinsky and others was written in a *Neo-Classical* style (or "new" classical). This was a return to the Classical principals of balance and form, and to music that did *not* describe any scene or emotion.

Composers have experimented with many ideas: some music is based on the laws of chance, some is drawn on graph paper, some lets the performers decide when or what to play, and some is combined with electronic or other sounds.

Popular music like jazz, country, folk, and rock & roll has had a significant impact on 20th century life and has influenced great composers like Aaron Copland and Leonard Bernstein. And the new technology of computers and electronic instruments has had a major effect on the ways music is composed, performed and recorded.

| 1900 | 1925 | 1950 | 1975 | 2000 |

ART & LITERATURE

- Robert Frost, author *(Stopping by Woods on a Snowy Evening)*
- Pablo Picasso, artist *(Three Musicians)*
- J.R.R. Tolkien, author *(The Lord of the Rings)*
- F. Scott Fitzgerald, author *(The Great Gatsby)*
- Andy Warhol, artist *(Pop art)*
- Salvador Dali, artist *(Soft Watches)*
- Norman Mailer, author *(The Executioner's Song)*
- John Steinbeck, author *(The Grapes of Wrath)*
- Ernest Hemingway, author *(For Whom the Bell Tolls)*
- Andrew Wyeth, artist *(Christina's World)*
- George Orwell, author *(1984)*

| 1900 | 1925 | 1950 | 1975 | 2000 |

WORLD EVENTS

- First airplane flight *(1903)*
- Television invented *(1927)*
- Berlin Wall built *(1961)*
- Destruction of Berlin Wall *(1989)*
- World War I *(1914-1918)*
- World War II *(1939–1945)*
- John F. Kennedy assassinated *(1963)*
- First radio program *(1920)*
- Civil rights march in Alabama *(1965)*
- First satellite launched *(1957)*
- Man walks on the moon *(1969)*
- Vietnam War ends *(1975)*
- Personal computers *(1975)*